Hi, little dog,
hi, fingers and toes—
we're awake!

Mama picks me up, holds me close, and sings me a good morning song.

Dada helps me make a delicious breakfast.

My baby wants some breakfast, too.

Uh-oh!

Some banana slices fell.

Uh-oh!

No, Marvin! You can't have my breakfast.

It's time to play
with my **ball!**

Dada has an owie—
that hurts. I help
him feel better.

"I love you, little dog."

"Woof woof," he says. He loves me, too.

Look at all the
bubbles in the tub!

Marvin does not
want a bath.

Bye bye, little dog.

This was such a
wonderful day.

Night-night.